The Egg Cookbook: Taking A Simple Ingredient and Turning it into Something Elegant

Disclaimer and Terms of Use: Effort has been made to ensure that the information in this book is accurate and complete, however, the author and the publisher do not warrant the accuracy of the information, text and graphics contained within the book due to the rapidly changing nature of science, research, known and unknown facts and internet. The Author and the publisher do not hold any responsibility for errors, omissions or contrary interpretation of the subject matter herein. This book is presented solely for motivational and informational purposes only.

Table of Contents

Egg Mushroom Salad

Ingredients:
- 2 C mushrooms
- 1 C chopped onions
- 1/3 C olive oil
- 3 T sour cream
- Chopped parsley
- 2-3 Hard Cooked eggs

Directions:

1. Fry your mushrooms, chopped onion and olive oil.
2. Mix the eggs with the sour cream and parsley and serve on rye toast.

Tea Eggs

Ingredients:
- Hard cooked eggs
- ½ C soy sauce
- 3 C water
- 4 star anise pods
- Tea bags
- orange peel

Directions:

1. Cook the eggs, and crack them but don't peel.
2. Simmer in a saucepan with remaining ingredients, for about an hour, than drain, peel and enjoy.

Egg Salad

Ingredients:
- Hard cooked eggs
- 3 T mayo
- 1 Chopped shallot
- 1 tsp white wine vinegar
- 1 T chopped tarragon
- Salt and pepper to taste

Directions:

1. Cook the eggs, chop and mix with the remaining ingredients and serve with sliced cucumbers.

Deviled eggs

Ingredients:
- Hard eggs
- 1 T sweet pickle relish
- 3 T mayo
- 1 tsp mustard
- Cayenne
- Salt and pepper to taste

Directions:

1. Make the eggs and scoop out the yolks.
2. Mix and mash the yolks with remaining ingredients and garnish with the seasonings.

Pickle Eggs

Ingredients:
- Hard cooked eggs
- Pickle beet juice

Directions:

1. Real simple, and great to eat.
2. Peel the eggs, and add them to a jar of the juice and let sit for about a week or so.
3. The longer it sits the bolder the flavor.

Eggs Scotty

Ingredients:
- Few eggs hard boiled/cooked
- Flour
- Panko
- Vegetable oil

Directions:

1. Boil the eggs, and peel.
2. Mix the sausage and eggs, encased.
3. Roll in four and panko and fry for a few minutes until crispy.

Eggs Hardy

Ingredients:
- 6 eggs
- ¼ C water (Cold)
- Lettuce

Directions:

1. Boil eggs in the water, and simmer. Serve over lettuce

Eggs Crispy

Ingredients:
- 2-3 eggs
- Flour
- Panko
- Vegetable oil

Directions:

1. Easy to make boil the eggs, and peel, roll in flour then panko, and fry in the vegetable oil (do not completely cover in oil)

Soldier Eggs

Ingredients:
- 4 eggs
- 1 C boiling water
- Salt and pepper to taste

Directions:

1. Boil the eggs in the water, cut top off eggs and season. Serve with Wheat toast

Scalloped potatoes

Ingredients:
- Hard cooked eggs
- Salt and pepper to taste
- Nutmeg
- 6 T milk
- Sour cream
- Boiled Potatoes
- 1 T flour
- Bread crumbs

Directions:

1. Cook the eggs and slice them and line the bottom of baking sheet with them.
2. Next add the potatoes, season with salt pepper and the nutmeg.
3. Next take care of the sour cream and milk, whisk with flour.
4. Pour the mix over everything in the baking dish Bake for 25 minutes or so.

Smoked Salmon

Ingredients:
- 3-4 eggs
- Whole wheat toast
- Smoked salmon

Directions:

1. Scramble the eggs, and top over the salmon and toast.

K Eggy

Ingredients:
- ½ C kimchi
- 2 scallions
- 1 T vegetable oil

Directions:

1. Sauté the kimchi and scallions, with vegetable oil.
2. Serve with two beaten eggs.

Egg Tortillas

Ingredients:
- Tortilla shells
- Eggs
- ½ C sliced onions
- Roasted peppers
- Vegetable oil
- Cheese
- Salsa

Directions:

1. Scramble the eggs, and cook peppers in the skillet with the onions and mix in the eggs, cheese then roll in the tortilla shells.

Eggy Muffins

Ingredients:
- Egg
- Salt and pepper to taste
- English muffin
- Melted cheddar

Directions:

1. Beat the egg or scramble it, whichever you prefer, set it in a mug, and microwave for about 30 seconds and serve on warm English muffin with cheese.

Creamy Eggs

Ingredients:
- 2 eggs whisked
- Heavy whipping cream
- Salt and pepper to taste
- 1 T butter

Directions:

1. Scramble the eggs with the whipping cream and butter, season with salt and pepper.

Meat and eggs

Ingredients:
- 1-2 scrambled eggs
- 1 oz. pastrami, sliced
- Feta cheese
- Scallions

Directions:

1. Lay pastrami down first, then your eggs, scallions and feta cheese

Biseggs

Ingredients:
- 1-2 scrambled eggs
- 1 T chopped chives
- 1 biscuit
- Cooked ham slice
- Cheese

Directions:

1. Open biscuit and add everything to the bottom, add top and you have a biscuit sandwich.

Saucy Eggs

Ingredients:

- Scrambled eggs
- 1/3 C cheddar cheese
- Jalapeño peppers, chopped

Directions:

1. Scramble the eggs in the skillet and add cheese and peppers in skillet and simmer on low heat.

Creamed Eggs

Ingredients:
- 2 T cream cheese
- 2 tsp chives
- 2 eggs
- Salt and pepper to taste

Directions:

1. Add butter to a skillet and in separate bowl add ingredients together and blend, add to skillet and cook.

Sugar and Spice Omelet

Ingredients:
- Traditional Omelet
- Pepper flakes
- 1 T jam
- Powdered sugar

Directions:

1. Start with a traditional omelet and add pepper flakes and fill with powdered sugar and jam/jelly

B&E salad

Ingredients:
- 1-2 poached eggs
- Crumbled bacon
- Chives
- Cheddar cheese

Directions:

1. Top eggs with bacon cheddar and chives and enjoy.

Fry Eggs

Ingredients:
- 1 C tater tots
- 1-2 scrambled eggs
- Bacon- crumbled
- Pepper flakes

Directions:

1. Mix everything together and enjoy.

Hell Eggs

Ingredients:
- Salsa or marinade
- 3-4 eggs

Directions:

1. Line baking dish with salsa or marinade, preheat oven to 350 degrees, whisk eggs and pour over salsa and bake for 10-12 minutes

Eggs and Spinach

Ingredients:
- Traditional omelet
- 3 T chopped asparagus
- 2 T feta cheese
- 2 T chopped spinach

Directions:

1. Make traditional omelet with these fillers.

Heart healthy omelet

Ingredients:
- ½ C sliced turkey
- 2 T salsa
- 4 egg whites
- Bacon

Directions:

1. Using olive oil use make omelet with these fillings.

Printed in Great Britain
by Amazon